The Walls Have Angels

The Walls Have Angels

Lesley Saunders

Published 2014 by Mulfran Press
2 Aber Street, Cardiff CF11 7AG
UK
www.mulfran.co.uk

The right of Lesley Saunders
to be identified as author of this work has been asserted in
accordance with the Copyright, Designs and Patents Act, 1988.

Poems © Lesley Saunders 2009, 2010, 2011, 2013, 2014

Cover photos courtesy of Dwain Comissiong
(www.flotion-photography.co.uk) who retains copyright.

ISBN 978-1-907327-23-0

All rights reserved. No part of this publication may be reproduced, stored in a retrieval system, or transmitted at any time or by any means, electronic, mechanical, photocopying, recording or otherwise without the prior permission of the copyright holder, except in the case of short extracts for inclusion in critical articles or reviews.

Printed by imprint**digital** in Devon [info@imprintdigital.net].

Acknowledgements

I am indebted to the proprietors of Acton Court for agreeing to create the part-time poetry residency during 2010–11.

I am also grateful to members of the Poetry Workshop, whose comments on early drafts of several of the poems were especially helpful. Helen McNeil was instrumental in giving shape to the collection.

An earlier version of 'The Power of Light' was published under a different title in *Poetry and Audience*, 2009. 'Tide' and 'Watch' were first published on the Manchester Poetry Prize website as part of the shortlisted portfolio for the 2010 poetry competition. 'Smalt' was published in *The Frogmore Papers* as first runner-up in the 2011 Frogmore Poetry Competition. 'Curatorial' was first published in *Salzburg Poetry Review* 2013.

Contents

I. Henry and Anne

Volta	11
Betrothal	12
A Private Performance	13
Nightshirt	14
Annunciation	16
Rampions	17
1534 – July, sex unknown	18
1535 – date unknown, sex unknown	19
1536 – January, male	20
Frost Point	21
Music for Two Keyboards	22
Oriel	23

II. The House

Psalms for the House	27

III. Watch

Gaudete	33
There Is No Australia	34
Watch	35
Tide	36
Curatorial	37
Smalt	38
Shudder	39
Stranger	40

IV. *The Walls Have Angels*

The Walls Have Angels	43
Through the Dimensions Disguised as Myself	44
The Power of Light	45
Out of the Blue	46
Enter The Dragon	47
Who Died	48
Afterlife	49

V.   Coda

Keepers	53

Notes

I. Henry and Anne

Volta
for Helen

> *During this step the man*
> *holds his partner in the air*
> *with the thigh of his free leg*
> *under her thighs.*

She leaps between his hands
like a salmon in a summer river,
her turn to fling herself up through

the glorious air towards the sun
and be held trembling in mid-heaven.
She's improvising wildly, throws

him with slow eyes, the flutter
of her fingers near the bare flesh
of his neck. He is the swan,

he will sink his full weight down
on her, he will come out of the sky
and cover her, he will draw blood.

Betrothal
for James Brookes

> *In 1528, the year after King Henry*
> *first proposed marriage, Anne Boleyn*
> *caught the sweating sickness.*

Caught but recovered from
like first love or pregnancy
and while it lasts bad enough
to rattle the king's calm

it puts her on her back like
the one vast and furious
fuck he would save for her,
the little death, the cure

she withholds, hot moist edicts
that would open her throat
and close the after-shocked eyes
in that gorgeous reeking head.

A Private Performance

After six years of courtship
Anne finally gave way to Henry
late in 1532, secretly in Calais

The alleluia years start here.
Immaterial whether the moon
is made of sea-mist or hoar-frost

– all eyes are on the stage-door.

Her walk-on is theatrical, her sleeves
have learnt their lines, how silk
has a dying fall all its own. *Le temps*

viendra, the curtain parts. Ah,

her stung face is enough: they hold
the wax lights nearer, crowding
the dark. His voice is bruised

as if the sea here were too narrow

or he were still her dancing bear.
Even if not all ships are vessels
this will be the night to remember.

The applause lasts into the small hours.

Nightshirt

> *'For a moment he seems like…*
> *a simpler form of himself'*
> Hilary Mantel, *Wolf Hall*

the space made by a room
with its furniture of sleep
and nightmares
is not a simple matter
of forms stacked between walls
or children wandering the streets

losing themselves
when there should have been owls
white and gifted as dreamlets

– no, the human body is altered
after marriage, it needs no
complication

although some mornings
we wake in a past room
so familiar is the window
and soft-footed

like the look of a pearl
that we feel we are
the kind of stuff
continuously inhabited

by light and memories
of light, winter birds
falling out of the sky
more spirit than flesh

but with full knowledge
of how on the sovereign body
this hand-stitched
finery of touch
is gentle as a seventh skin
a veil between worlds

for though silk must have its weight
in running water
and linen its wrappings
and swaddlings like a bride
her trousseau of birdsong

here in the sleep laboratory
of accidents and ceremonies
there is only the yoga of clear light
the sleeping lord

Annunciation

> *'By daily proof you shall me find*
> *To be to you both loving and kind'*
> Note to Henry written
> by Anne in her *Book of Hours*

At each window kneels a woman who waits,
her face contemplative as glass. It is the look
of one who knows herself from within,
who can read between the lilies, and bleeds.

The angels peel themselves from their walls,
in search of a molten shade of blueish-gold
they will not find. These rich hours like rubies
are not set in stone. Every month slows to a year.

Rampions

Her lust is for rampions,
their fat flesh-like roots
white as a little one's wrists,
a passion that's sated only

by nightfall and her full-bellied
dreams. She'd stoop to theft
if she could, lamb's lettuce
from the rampant witch-garden,

the poor women's spell-salad,
round blond baby-fruit hidden
in quiet-leaved secretive places.
The sun is pale as moonlight

as the sickness rises. They bring
her buttermilk, comfort food.
She holds out her aching arms
to the crammed room, craving.

1534 – July, sex unknown

As if the whole ocean-bed
had stirred in its sleep
      something faraway
      and not nearly finished

steepened into pain like a wall
not to be waded through
      even in dreams and what
      she imagined was land

is a leap from the bridge
      a shoe lost at sea.

1535 – date unknown, sex unknown

Like a painting on glass,
a portrait of light stalled
    in a rose-gold frame,

it is pure conjecture,
from moment to moment
    it could fracture

into a weep of ash-petals
and pipit-bones along this
    faint hairline of dark.

1536 – January, male

This is how shame takes
its exquisite shapes, its
    frond-like inscriptions

    on tall fiery windows,

its blue opalescences,
its small face cupped
    in a feverish flower,

    tendernesses

all painted from life, all
possibilities finely
    crossed through,

    nothing made new.

Frost Point

This not speaking is a new intimacy. Its music
is pure like a tune of refrains played on glass,
no impromptu verse to urge the story on.

His silence is winter. She composes herself,
white-faced lady-in-waiting, ghost in the pane
where a dove keeps diving into its icy likeness.

Even the ink is freezing over, nibs splintering
against its crust. White ferns scrawl up the window
and her italics stutter softly into blackened frost.

Music for Two Keyboards

i.

She was sky-walking in the garden, stepping through
    the sorrow of clouds. The song in her head held

its wisteria note for the length of a question
    like a lament for someone not dead, till all she wanted

was to sail her house down the river and into the sea.
    These are the grey places that survive in the mind,

the lost tune she thought she could never dance to,
    though its other names are still bright with regret,

the evergreen marches between human heartlands
    mourning old wrongs. She was singing a love song

for truth but it falls from the air in shatters,
    the small sheer sounds of all her life in front of her.

ii.

    The small sheer sounds of all his life in front of him
are the truth as it falls from the air in shatters

    mourning old wrongs. He was singing a love song
of the evergreen marches between human heartlands,

    though its other names are still bright with regret,
the lost tune he thought he would never dance to.

    These are the grey places that survive in the mind,
while he sails his house down the river and into the sea

    like a lament for someone not dead: all he wanted
was its wisteria note held for the length of a question;

    the song in his head was the sorrow of clouds.
Sky-walking in the garden, he was stepping right through.

Oriel

The light being winterlight
finds out each muse
of glass, every
filament of metal woven

into tiny brocades, the flying
diamantes of dust, all
the discarded rain-creatures
and fish-scales,

the last sullen river-pearl;
then lays itself out across the floor
silently as a counterpane,
faithfully as a knife-edge.

II. *The House*

Psalms for the House

i.

Like a thin-faced child
trying to be nobody
eating off winter bird-tables

the house hides from itself
stealing light from the afternoons
writing all over the walls.

ii.

A shack of rock
battened on a lease of rock:

ravines of shadows
like wolves or heresies;

a moat choked
with the once of a house,
its knick-knacks and drabs;

a high-pitched rainbow
like a pageant of hallows;

the way the heart knocks;
and the doves.

iii.

After the long journeys
and the epic snowfalls
comes this pale creeping

like the remains of an eye.
A tree of single silver,
everything bides

within the parish of its care,
no need yet for action
or decision. Drift in light.

iv.

And then the talk turns
    to visitors
how the medicinal air
    and the walled light
will take them gently
    under the elbows
lift them clear
    of gravity
so they come floating
    across the orchard
and one will tell you
    how her daughter
ran to greet her
    as she stepped
long dead from grief
    into the waiting
arms of the garden.

v.

Footsteps of wet.
Troubled or rebellious children
with prominent eyes
that see better at night.
Clairvoyants whose amazing
sense of smell.
Couples sharing no more
than a glass of bedside water.
Book-moths with Latin names
as alibis. Atmospheres of violet.
Migrants, spinsters and enchanters.
Cinnamons from Bristol. Eisenglimmers.
Scattered lives. The benison
of ghosts.

vi.

In the weeks before spring
the trees start perfecting
their harp-music

all their grace-notes
held so long in the pale air
they might be cut-outs

of birds or first leaves,
ghosts of an orchard
perfumed with nests

and the purl of courtesies,
a hall of weathers
where the small lives

of collared doves and russets
might be sung in the unfurnished
spaces under the skin

green jesus rising.

vii.

Just this:
    the exquisite mystery
of his disappearance
    that day last year
into the mineral and air
    of his final self
the lit candles like

delicate lupins behind
    his shut eyelids
and the slight sense of
    mistaken identity
each time the daughters
catch sight of their
vivid altered selves.

viii.

    Re-enactment: a bletted
        choke-apple with traces
            of habitation. A leak

of dark sweetness,
      scenes from married life.
          In the middle distance,

tapestry of cow in clover.
      After the hunt, nest-like
          civilities; a held-in bliss.

The old English virtues,
      medlar, mulberry, quince.
          This great munificence.

III. Watch

Gaudete

Season of taper lights
and ice fairs, a moon

no more than a nail paring,
lead white and radiant

as a dancer starving
for the pharma of touch,

her bird bones an x-ray
of separation. Reach up

and hold her fingertip.
Its weight will amaze you.

There Is No Australia

There is no Australia
though there are interiors like continents painted with earth's
hurts and burnt umbers, then fading heraldically at sunset to the slow
pains of coral and roses, objects of desire all facing seawards

There is no Australia
though there are sleeves woven with serpents of wisdom,
there are scarlets slashed and garish as a lizard's gape, dragons of brightness
splitting the night skies, there are gunboats and brocades

There is no Australia
though there are rooms glimpsed within rooms, triple mirrors
and light from long-ago windows passing through figures who swim
for dear life in the cool emerald air like nomads or tree-surgeons

There is no Australia
though like vast paranoias of the zodiac there are orreries
encased in chrysoprase and the king's spies everywhere, there are children
trying to tiptoe to Beverleyham from the other side of the world

There is no Australia
though there are fields and fields of cloth of gold, ivoried rooks
and intricate wargames, A to Zs of the wastes beyond the north wind,
portolanos of the unconscious as hot and wet as Kumari Kandam

though for the moment there is no Australia

Watch

> *'several graffiti of ships*
> *are near the east entrance'*
> Rediscovering Acton Court
> *and the Poyntz Family*

In their hearts they are the island nation,
race of isolates, even the inland tribes
who have only the dream of sea are obsessed

with horizons and the voluptuous possibility
of ships. Unassailable as cliffs they have gone
to the end of the earth to the edge of the land

to see for themselves how war looks like a sail.
On the outskirts of towns there are artichoke beds
and the serene mooring on a slow-moving Frome

and after lights out the late night shipping news.
Still their eyes have the scrimped sheen of sea-glass
and in the simple dawn they bandage their hearts

like world-forsakers against the bottomless crossing
through fog to the outcrop, atoll, holm.

Tide

The long gallery has a frieze
of biblical text in Latin

They arrive by night, coming in like shoals
    or spies on the grey tide. By first light
they have vanished into the hinterlands

where tables in lamplit homesteads are set
    in readiness for the unwinding of cloths,
the raising of life from the dead, the reciting

of chapter and verse behind closed doors.
    In the begynnynge was that worde,
its full light falling now on all surfaces

and sills, the glistening milk-pail, the porringers
    kept for best. Someone sits with both hands
cupped at her ears, each syllable sipped

like old barleywine. The good books
    will be read and read till their spines break;
single leaves will be had by heart or sewn

into seams, *for they shalbe called the chyldren*
    of God. Across the water, a condemned man
requests a candle, walks into a sea of flame.

Curatorial

> *'the tremendous
> symbolic dignity of things.'*
> Lindsay Clarke,
> *The Chymical Wedding*

House of muses whose only exhibits
are rain-soaked displays of daylight,
this is not what we came for,

this elusive arrangement of doorways,
these bared walls magnificently untranslated.
We expected something,

a flute made from the bone of a goose,
or china dishes the dead have touched
that season they wore their flesh

nonchalantly as sleeves,
leaving cups hanging by a finger, bowls
filling to the brim with a room's breath –

touchables, like the sour plums
seared from their branches
by a late-summer meteor-shower

or love-letters pushed nightly
under the door by an invisible hand.
We wanted the nuptial devotions

of tables laid with worn silver,
a decorative chafing dish handle:
shape-shifters, soothsayers.

We were dreaming of thimbles,
we wanted a cure of souls.

Smalt

Did he see it coming, that blue?
It was more like air than anything.
Could he trust it, not to get too close,

      to stay in the realm of ultramarines,

the flat-out fields reclaimed from sea?
Not to leave him alone, untouchable
in the glass-like condition of yellow?

      I am an only child but the house

does not want me to wear black.
It loves the open throats
of ox-blood, rose, the aestival

      visitations of gold. The blue

was something else: the cool of wall
against a woman's back, the linen
weight of her hem, and the light itself

      material as the jug of warm milk

in a corner. I remember the small
luminous time of settling a child
safely in bed, the beauty of the body's

      response to dusk and its sleeping-suit

of selfhood: so easily overlooked,
like a species of unregarded flower
or the way evening in a kitchen

      briefly illumines a loved face,

that we are in danger of losing them
and making no record of the loss.
Faces on a simple blue ground, ghosts

      of the future. Did he see it coming?

Shudder

> *'An aura... almost tangibly gold*
> *can be perceived around the performer'*
> Anthony Rooley, *Performance*

As if lightning will strike, the house
has lit its candles of lilies, prepared
        its concert of sunsets, the long present

hanging on an out-breath, unsayable
name of god in the mouth, tongue-tied
        wafer. As if to stop the music altogether.

Which anyway creeps smokily into
the body from some downstairs bar
        like a struggle for custody, a private party,

the lute's boat floating us along an exiled
river. Here in the castello the acoustic's
        good, all the quiet notes trying to find

someone to kill. What do you want? What
are you doing here? Praying to get lost in
        these lost moments, pure reflex. Slow

down. Slow it down. Simple gift-givers,
love and music travelling the road
        as far as the source of song or fire,

though some drive for hours and
never arrive. You'd like to know
        everything: the theogony of stars,

metals in transit like young kings
bright with battle; salvific chords
        in the old dry style; new schools

of melancholy. O westron wynde
show us the way, Saturday night fevers,
        movements of the soul in vivacious flesh:

and now comes the hawk swooping
for its sparrow like a grace or rapture
        out of the blue, turning you gold.

Stranger
for Laura

> '... 'Tis as like you
> As cherry is to cherry.'
> Henry VIII, V.1. 168–9.

> 'I made this, I have forgotten
> And remember.'
> T.S. Eliot, *Marina*.

before the moment of recognition
with the light behind you
blue as eyes
the word daughter lies cradled

in the hollow of the question
a conversation he has yet to have
with himself, the one thing
he must give away to get back

and for this he is reading all
the research on fathers, their heroism
and shipwrecks
how they survived by going mad
until music could be brought on board
to restore them

or as if by saying the name of a child over
and over like the surf on granite rocks
at the bottom of the world
or by riding deeper into the forest to stand
inside the roaring silence of pine trees
hiding-place of so many deaths

he could find this against-all-odds nativity
this passage through anger and danger
for which daughter is the only password

and though the scene is unclear at this point
the moated house an island lost in fog
go not till he speak

IV. *The Walls Have Angels*

The Walls Have Angels

The walls have angels

Who come at us airily
bringing fire with them
in the shape of rivers

Who manifest themselves
through the mineral light
of chrysanthemums
the earthly powders
of copper and bronze

Whose Latin is fluent but mute

Who are visible in attitudes
of rarity especially
to young men in the afternoon

Who shine like the rain

Who gild their eyelids *ma non troppo*
and never panic
but rejoice unbearably

Who stand at our backs
pointing spears
like a troop of hallelujahs
or the thirteen moons of Neptune
almoners and hypnagogues

Bringers of pity and shock

Through the Dimensions Disguised as Myself

Shot. Like silk or
Turkish pearlglimmer,

gorge de pigeon.
Flocking into your room

at three a.m.
I make you think

of words like breasted,
nestling, threat.

Between the lines I am what is written
and as you move towards

the threshold
I turn my palest blue

in the direction of purple,
accipiter.

The Power of Light

What if I came alone, brought
        no friends. Spoke without notes

in front of all these silences,
        parting the air with my arms

to make way for the arrival of forests,
        a glimpse of the interior.

Stood my ground like the sound
        of water, its welling and emptying

on which the earth rests, nothing
        end-gained, pre-empted. Let go

of my own ownings precious as
breath. If by so doing I could

forget how to breathe,
        being made of beating wings,

the oxygens of long-legged roads,

                        slow light.

Out of the Blue

It always begins with a horse, you said,

no reins or saddle, but a headstrong turn
towards the sea and into the sun, a canter
along the wheat-blond shore like the horizon
back home, Kansas, Arkansas, heat-hazed
and untamed. Comes a dancer

out of the Gloucestershire bluebell woods
blue-veiled with whatever it takes
to get to the truth. Some one has rubbed
the silk of the air till its hair stands on end,

in King Henry's room someone has walked
through the firewall to the far side
of Prussian, a bad-fairy blue but still
this end of visible, not earthable, wired.

It will begin again with a horse, that symbol
of faithfulness, inventor of telegrams
and electro-shock therapy, it will arrive
this time as cobalt, as tigers
riderless and riddled with sapphires,

it will be lightning striking an Iowa of sky.

Enter The Dragon

For a year the room and its window
have been steeped
in sky-blue
and all its cleansing weathers,

the mauve walking alongside
until turquoise opens the door.
Those who come from the realm of spirits
need no priest

only the shaman-painter
who with her hog-hair brushes
and canvas drum summons
the horse, horse

in its dragon form
arriving out of the east,
north, west, south.
The air is suddenly bee-yellow,

peony-red, aflame:
there is more to this world than this world,
more to sovereignty
than a fat king's ransom.

And, although nothing is scorched
beyond the halo of our stare,
the field of the cloth of gold
is rising again like a burning bush,

is rushing with nasturtiums,
sackbuts, salamanders:
Shogun, Khan, Inca, Maharajah, the old
majesties gathering.

Who Died

Red smoke
floats on the blank air.

It has a dark rustle like leaves
that have left their tree

and are veining the stones.
Yet as it travels

by hearsay and ship's talk
it sings,

it is hackled with anger,
it is the wind lifting the tarpaulin,

still burning,
scented with coals.

Afterlife

Silence falls evenly like light
    clear as a gallery of glass
        a whole time of it

as if the massed sky
    weightless as theatre
        had become the shape

inside the stone, an interior
    echoing with half-names
        Kat Jem Bet Liz

whose fading lasts and lasts
    like the phantom pain
        of lost wings, dismantled

rooms. Then a sudden
    draught on the fine hairs
        of my skin: a house

grieving for its court, death
    on intimate terms
        with the king.

＊*V. Coda*

Keepers

> *'[the house] was to be returned to
> private ownership and use once repaired...'*
> Paul Drury,
> 'The Rescue of Acton Court'

Finder of the wish-bones,
hinge-maker, linch-pin,
custodian of the finials,

after the crowds have left
your old house turns to gold.
At the door the last visitor

must slough his dead skins
like a disreputable coat
and wait for the music.

Keeper of the small finds
– winters of green glass, lesser
starworts, the broken end-part

of a physician's syringe
for use at sea – your halls
are full of sky,

its merciful white birds
seep through gapes
in the oak like sweepings

of female pins. We
can only guess who was here,
a flower-arranger perhaps,

dog-walker, auditor, star-
gazer: keepers of the iron
keys, the phoenix, the flame.

Notes

As writer-in-residence at Acton Court over a two-year period, I felt impelled to find connections between the hauntingly beautiful house, the quality of its atmosphere and appearance, and events that might or might not have taken place here in the recent or distant past. Acton Court is an early Tudor manor house and grounds on the outskirts of Iron Acton, near Yate in south-west England. In 1535 King Henry VIII and his second wife, Anne Boleyn, were touring the west country with the royal court: the owner, Nicolas Poyntz, was obliged to add a magnificent new East Wing to the existing moated house to accommodate them. In the late seventeenth century the place was converted into a farmhouse. The East Wing has remained substantially intact, however, and – thanks to English Heritage which funded its restoration in the late twentieth century – now survives as a unique Tudor building. Visit www.actoncourt.com

Chronology in such an environment seems softly layered and interconnecting rather than compartmentalised into specific periods and centuries, and the poems do not make strong distinctions of time and history. Nonetheless it would have been odd not to be particularly struck by the Tudor connection. As we know, King Henry VIII's 'great matter' was the production of a male heir. It doesn't take much guesswork to imagine that Anne Boleyn, having held Henry off for six years, was preoccupied thereafter by the urgent need to present him with a son. Whatever the affairs of state dominating their conscious thoughts during the short time Henry and Anne stayed at Acton Court during their Summer Progress, biology must have been the unignorable undercurrent.

Volta
This Renaissance dance was described, with dance notations, by a 16th century French cleric – writing under the pen-name Thoinot Arbeau – in his book *Orchésographie*.

There is a passing reference in the poem to Thomas Wyatt's poignant sonnet, 'Whoso list to hunt', which ends with the words 'and wild for to hold'.

Betrothal
The dedicatee James Brookes is the author of *The English Sweats*, published by Pighog Press 2009.

A Private Performance
Le temps viendra – 'the time will come' – is said to have been written by Anne Boleyn in the first book she owned, a Book of Hours from Bruges.

The magnificence of the court, which was a mobile entity – Henry VIII possessed some sixty residences – consisting of possibly up to a thousand people, paradoxically meant there was very little personal and private space, even (or especially) for the King.

Nightshirt
Henry made it fashionable to sleep in a nightshirt – however, according to Herbert Norris in Tudor Costume and Fashion, 'No bridegroom or bride wore a nightshirt.... When Henry wished to repudiate his marriage with the Lady Anne of Cleves he declared he was never without one at night; in other words, the marriage was not consummated.'

Annunciation
Anne's message to Henry – the epigraph to the poem – was handwritten beneath an illuminated illustration of the Annunciation, when the angel Gabriel tells the Virgin Mary she will bear a son.

Rampions
According to the website www.botanical.com *A Modern Herbal*, 'rampion, formerly regularly cultivated in English kitchen gardens, and much valued as a wholesome esculent vegetable, is... still much cultivated in France, Germany and Italy, and occasionally here, for the roots which are boiled tender like parsnips and eaten hot with a sauce... Drayton names it among the vegetables and pot-herbs of the kitchen garden, in his poem *Polyolbion*, and there is a reference to it in the slang of Falstaff, showing how generally it was in cultivation in this country in Shakespeare's time... The plant figures in one of Grimm's tales, the heroine, Rapunzel, being named after it, and the whole plot is woven around the theft of rampions from a magician's garden.' Alison Lurie (in *The New York Review of Books*, LV, 7, 40–43) says that the tale of Rapunzel usually 'begins with two intense cravings: that of a pregnant woman for a plant that grows in a garden next door, and that of a witch for a girl child.'

The learned and witty anthropologist of everyday life, Margaret Visser, tells us (in *Much Depends on Dinner*, Penguin Books 1986) that vegetables 'in our culture have always been considered women's food'; real men need red meat:

'Owre Englische native cannot lyve by Roots,
By water, herbys or such beggarye baggage...
Give Englische men meate after their old usage,
Beiff, Mutton, Veale, to cheare their courage'

(William Forrest, 1548, quoted by Margaret Visser, page 222.)

1534, 1535, 1536
It is documented that Anne had a miscarriage in the summer of 1534, possibly a second in 1535 and certainly another early in 1536: that last pregnancy was advanced enough for Anne, and all the court, to know the infant would have been a boy. Four months later – less than a year after their sojourn at Acton Court – Anne herself would be dead, accused by many of being a witch and a heretic and beheaded at the command of her husband on charges of high treason, adultery with several named men and incest with her brother.

Music for Two Keyboards
'Sky-walking', I was told by Harriet (a young lady who knows about these things), is when you walk looking down into a mirror held just under your nose, so you feel as if you're walking through the sky.

The poem was 'given' to me by the lutenist Matthew Spring, with whom I performed in an evening of words and music at Acton Court on 1st August 2010 and who told me about the type of musical piece composed for lute or keyboard, known as a dump (or domp). These are most probably laments and several examples survive from the 16th and early 17th centuries: the earliest example is My Lady Carey's Dompe (*circa* 1525) for keyboard or cittern, printed in Stafford Smith's *Musica Antiqua*, ii, 470, from a MS. in the British Museum. Lady Carey was Mary Boleyn, sister to Anne.

'Dump' is thought to be derived either from the Dutch word 'domp' (meaning 'haze' or 'dullness'), or from 'tump', an English dialect word for tomb. By the early 16th century it had come to mean a melancholy state as well as a mournful piece of music: 'Dump – plural, dumps – is a very respectable monosyllable, of ancient origin, and belonging to a family members of which are found in every country of Northern Europe – in every land, that is to say, where man and nature come into conflict and the human has a hard time of it.' Joseph Bennett, *The Musical Times and Singing Class Circular*, Vol. 42, No. 695 (Jan. 1, 1901), pp. 13–15.

There Is No Australia
Australia was not discovered by the Europeans until 1606 (under subsequent colonial law it was declared *'terra nullius'*, 'belonging to no-one').

Tide
William Tyndale began his work of singlehandedly translating the New Testament into English from the original Greek and Hebrew in 1524. His 'four shilling' bible was hugely popular with the people and editions were smuggled in their thousands into England from Europe wrapped in bales of cloth. Anne Boleyn had her own personal copy. The Lord Chancellor, Sir Thomas More, was outraged that Tyndale was 'putting the fire of scripture into the language of ploughboys', though his concern was as much about Tyndale's alleged German Lutheranism as about his language. The bibles were destroyed by the authorities as soon as they were found and in 1536 Tyndale was burned at the stake as a heretic. Three years later Henry VIII issued the so-called Great Bible, the first English edition to be authorised.

Curatorial
The artefacts excavated from the Acton Court site include various household objects (such as those italicised in the poem) and pieces of masonry found in the moat; they are not on display at Acton Court, being held in storage at the Bristol City Museum. For a comprehensive scholarly account of the architecture, topography and contents of the house, see Rodwell, K. and Bell, R. (eds), *Acton Court: The Evolution of an Early Tudor Courtier's House*, published by English Heritage in 2004.

Smalt
Smalt, a finely ground blue glass, came into use for painting in the 15th century; Hans Holbein – court painter to Henry VIII – used it, mixed with balsam and resin rather than oil, as the background in many of his portraits. It produces a vivid jewel-like blue with a translucence and deep richness. The poem owes its origin to a photograph of one of the women from the Hungerford Household re-enactment troupe: she's dressed in blue and white homespun, with a cap on her head, and sits in the kitchen of Acton Court as though she has been there for the last four hundred years.

Shudder
The 'shudder' as an aesthetic idea cropped up twice in what I was reading in the summer of 2010; first in a piece by Frank Kermode on TS Eliot's literary criticism and his notion of 'the horror, or even the beauty, of a body's response to violent stimulus' ('Eliot and the shudder', London Review of Books, 32, 9, 13–16); and then in a piece by Greil Marcus ('The yarragh', Guardian Review, 5 June 2010, 18) on the way the music of Van Morrison causes 'a shudder [to] pass through the body... I hear Van Morrison's whole 45-year professional career as a quest for that shudder'. 'It's about getting out of one's way so the soul can be heard, I suppose' – Van Morrison, quoted in Los Angeles Times, 9 January 2009. When I read a selection of these poems to an audience at Acton Court, I felt that the house itself was listening, and the shudder passed through me.

Stranger
The first epigraph is from *Henry VIII*, one of Shakespeare's very last plays, and is from the scene where the nurse tells Henry that the longed-for boy Anne has just given birth to is a girl. Often in Shakespeare's late plays daughters appear as figures of consolation, redemption. *Pericles* is another of these, and the prolonged recognition / reconciliation scene, in Act V, Scene i, between Pericles and his daughter Marina is deeply and enduringly affecting. Even though he will not speak to her she determines to stay, and sings to him. The last line of the poem is taken from Marina's speech at this critical juncture. The second epigraph is taken from T. S. Eliot's poem 'Marina'.

Leaving aside all these literary references, however, the poem recalls the fact that Anne left Henry with a daughter who went on to become one of the greatest of all English monarchs – so it is essentially a response to the time-space continuum that is Acton Court.

Through the Dimensions Disguised As Myself
The last word of the poem, accipiter, is Latin for hawk, and I think of a hawk as a streak of brightness that bursts through from another dimension...

Keepers
The epigraph is taken from the introductory chapter in the book about Acton Court cited above (Rodwell and Bell, eds).